In the Waiting:

What to Do When You Are Going Through

by

Joycelyn Allen

DORRANCE
PUBLISHING CO
EST. 1920
PITTSBURGH, PENNSYLVANIA 15238

Dorrance Publishing Co
585 Alpha Drive
Suite 103
Pittsburgh, PA 15238
Visit our website at *www.dorrancebookstore.com*

ISBN: 978-1-6853-7179-1
eISBN: 978-1-6853-7722-9

I have been through a lot wanting to take my own life and sometimes didn't feel like I had anyone or I didn't want to be a burden to others. I looked to God for my inspiration to keep going and never giving up. I continued to read the word and believe in the words I was reading/hearing, just knowing that God loves me, Jesus died for me and He would never leave me no matter what I'm going through, and I can always talk to Him. Life is kind of like a waiting game. I learned to wait and be patient for my circumstances to change, for me to change, and for whatever I was praying for. I also learned to accept how things are going now, to accept myself, and accept my past. I wrote this book as an inspiration to others who may have gone or are currently going through difficult situations. Pain is pain and none of it feels good no matter what form it comes in.

I dedicate this book to my three beautiful children. I love them so much. They are one of the reasons why I am still here. I cherish my children because they keep me going, they are my favorite company. I couldn't imagine a life without them. Also, my mother, who was always there for me, Joyce Marie.

Contents

Chapter 1

Almost Destroyed but God Restored

Many people do not know much about me, they know of me. Even the ones that think they know me do not. I would like to take this time to apologize to anyone I may have hurt in the past, friends, family, etc. If you ever thought that I was acting funny, thought that I think that I am better than you, or anytime I saw you and did not speak, it was never anything personal towards any of you. It was things that I was going through and I did not know how to deal with them. Years back I was a mess. I was drowning in depression for years. I had to learn no matter what I was going through, I could not take it out on the people around me. It took me a while to learn that. That is not okay. I just want to share a little about me, a small portion of the things that I've been through and how God have brought me through the things that were meant to destroy me. I've been through a lot. I will show you how God can use anybody and how He can turn you into a completely different person, if you let Him.

One of the things some people see when they look at me is beauty. But that is not what I see. Please know that when I refer to my looks I am not thinking highly of myself. I've never been the one to let my looks go to my head. When I looked in the mirror I did not see beauty. I saw pain, my mistakes, and wrong decisions. Never be jealous of someone for what they have, who they are, or what they look like. You don't know what they may be going through behind closed doors, and you don't know what they had to do to get what they have. So please do not be jealous of me or anyone else. For the majority of my life I hated myself, my past, I hated everything about myself. I think up until last year I began to love myself. Just last year. I had a lot of unhappy days. I always kept myself dolled up to hide the ugliness in my heart of the self-hatred that I had for my own self.

Some things that make people hate themselves:

- The family that they were born into
- The things that they been through
- The way people have treated them/made them feel like they are nothing
- Shame/embarrassment
- Failures
- Appearance

Now we all know that everybody is going through something. It's in the Bible that we will all have trials and tribulations. Some people may go through things way worse than what we went through. Or, we may have had it worse than someone else. Who's to say? Pain is pain and none of it feels good. Nobody wants to go through something that is going to break them.

I do not mind sharing with you the things that I have been through.

When I was younger, around ten or twelve, my dad did drugs and alcohol. Almost every weekend he would hit on my mom and just cause chaos. This went on for years. My dad often said things that he shouldn't have said to me and my siblings as children. Things that would persuade our minds to make us think differently about our mother. Even as a child I knew what to believe and what not to believe. Even still the things he said got confusing because I didn't want to believe that my dad would lie to me. Not only did my dad do drugs; he was never there for me when I needed him to be. My dad didn't know anything about me. I don't ever remember him even trying to get to know me. Believe it or not, sometimes when a parent is or parents are not in a child's life it can cause damage to a child. I know we have all seen that show *My 600-lb. Life*. The majority of those people's moms or dads had left them or passed away. Even though I haven't lived with my dad in over 20 years, the traumatic events and him not being there for me still bother me till this day. He is still alive and I still love him, always will, he is my dad, and I have forgiven him for the pain he has caused years ago.

Also, at the age of 19 my brother passed away at the age 10. He died from an asthma attack. At the time I really didn't understand why my brother had to die. I didn't even believe it at first. I just had to see his body to believe it. I struggled with that for a while. My first response was shock, disbelief, then grief. But I had to realize that my brother was really sick, and he said himself the day that he died that he was tired of being sick and he wanted God to take him. And that's exactly what happened that day. I get so sad thinking of him because as the years go by I can't remember that many details about him. I don't remember what he sounded like, I don't really remember laughing and playing with him, which I know I did. But I don't have any of those memories anymore. That saddens me deeply. I miss him so much. Please cherish and love on your loved ones while they are here because when they are gone, they are gone. The last thing I said to my brother was not nice. I was getting ready for work and on my way out the door he tells me bye. I told him to shut up. I was upset about who knows what. I had no way of knowing that he would die the next day or I would have never said that. My last words to him, wow, that hurt me for so long. This is why we should never take our anger out on other people when they are not the reason we are upset. Took me a long time to finally forgive myself for that.

At the age of twenty-three, I got married and was divorced at the age of twenty-six. When you marry young and you expect to spend the rest of your life with someone and your marriage falls apart before your eyes, it will break you. It sure did break me, I was broken for years. I didn't think that I would ever stop loving that man. Once you put your all into someone or a marriage and that marriage ends and that person is no longer there, what are you left with? Nothing. It left me with nothing. I was depressed for a very long time. I was depressed because I only wanted to be married once, I was embarrassed, and I was very much in love with him. We had a lot together, did a lot together. I didn't want what we had to end. But it did. God warned me that the marriage was going to end. I had three dreams that it would end. The first dream was a dream about our wedding rehearsal. I dreamed that it would be a disaster and it was. I believe everything happened like it did in the dream and I couldn't do anything to stop it. Second dream I dreamed he put me out the house and said that it was over. Third dream I dreamed that he was running from me and I could never catch him. After I had that dream I asked him would he ever leave me, he said, "No, I would never do that, I don't want to get a divorce." Even though he stated that we would not get a divorce, God was preparing me for what was about to happen. Not much longer after that the marriage ended, I didn't think that my heart would ever stop hurting. God eventually healed me from those wounds.

Now if the first three things didn't destroy me, this last thing almost did. I suffer from fibromyalgia and bursitis of both hips. If you do not know what that is let me explain. Fibromyalgia is an autoimmune disease where the body attacks itself. Bursitis is inflammation, pain, swelling, and stiffness in the hips, elbow, shoulders, and knees. People who suffer from fibromyalgia have pain all over. From your face, arm, back, neck, shoulders, legs, thighs, feet, and butt. They also experience fatigue, nausea, trouble sleeping, headaches, depression, anxiety, brain fog, trouble concentrating, remembering things, severe stomach pain, constipation, etc. Sometimes I get so nauseated that I want to vomit, I dry heave or just plain have the urge to vomit but it never happens. It's very mind boggling, to think you may vomit but nothing comes about. When I first was diagnosed with this I almost lost my mind several times. Going through so much pain caused me to have anxiety and depression. Not only was I dealing with life challenges, going through a divorce, being a mom, working a stressful job, going to classes, etc. Also going through all of this plus dealing with physical pain was so much to deal with. Waking up stiff and hurting and going to bed hurting will make you depressed. Sure, I took pain meds but after a while the medicine stopped working, and I had to suffer through the pain most days. Sometimes I would feel like I got beat up or I felt like I got hit by a truck. Times I hurt so bad I would call certain people and tell them I don't think I will wake up in the morning and I would give them all my debit card information. Also telling them who I wanted to have my children. Other times I would say to God please just take me now if this is what my life is to be.

I never thought that I would get past depression. I was broken for so long, I had to remember that the Lord is close to the broken-hearted and he saves those who are crushed in spirit (Psalm 34:18). But when He is finished breaking us down the first thing we need to do is get back up. Accept what you have been through, and know that it does not define you. Take a step back and look how much stronger you have become.

These four things were meant to destroy me, mentally, physically, and emotionally, but I am still here. I did not let fibromyalgia win or the other things that broke me. God kept me and he changed my mind every time. So many times, I wanted to take my own life. I had to make up in my own mind, "For God I live and for God I will die." Not because I wanted to, but I had to make up my mind to live for God no matter what I was going through. I heard somebody once say, "God gives the toughest battles to the strongest soldiers."

Isaiah 12:2: He gives power to the faint and him who has no might He increases strength.

Please know that you are loved, God loves you.

If you are struggling with loving yourself or accepting yourself, you have to love yourself first before you can love anybody else. If you don't love yourself, how or why do expect other people to love you? Love you for you, and accept you for you, no matter what you have done or what you have been through. God still loves you. So please forgive yourself and love yourself.

John 15:13: Greater love no one has one than this, than to lay down one's life for his friends.

Jesus died so that we may not perish but have everlasting life. If that is not love, then I don't know what is.

God says, "I am good, you are loved." It took me a while to get this.

Philippians 4:19: And my God shall supply all your needs according to his riches and glory by Christ Jesus.

James 4:8: Draw near to God, and He will draw near to you.
Isaiah 43:2: When you pass through the waters I will be with you, and through the rivers, they shall not overflow you, when you walk through the fire you shall not be burned, nor shall the flame scorch you.

Deuteronomy 31:8: It is the Lord who goes before you, He will be with you; He will not fail you or forsake you. Do not fear or be dismayed.

I read all of these scriptures before but they never really sunk in. Sometimes when going through depression you forget about who you are and who God is. That's how the enemy will trick your mind, by planting a seed that you are nobody and that nobody loves you. What greater love than what Jehovah provides.

When these scriptures finally clicked, and I realized who I was and who God is in my life, my life changed. I became happy, depression left with a quickness, things don't bother me like they used to. I have patience, slow to anger. I am truly happy with who I am and with all that I have. When you learn how to give God everything, spend more time with Him, pray more, and read the word every day and worship God in spirit and in truth, there is no way your life can remain the same.

I thank God for saving me.

> Dear God,
> Thank you for keeping me for the times I did not want to be kept. Thank you for giving me breath, the times when I did not want to breathe. Thank you for keeping me alive all the times I wanted to die. Thank you, God, so much for hearing my cry. Thank you for bringing me through all the torture that I caused myself. Thank you for providing a way out, when I thought there was no way. Thank you, God, I can never repay for the things you done for me. Lord, I thank you for the peace of mind that you have blessed me with. Lord, I thank you. In Jesus' name, I pray, Amen.

Daddy Issues

Some people may think okay, your dad wasn't that active in your life, so what? I know that by my dad not being there it was very hard to get over. It took a long time to get over. It really hurts me that I am not a priority to him then or now. It was always painful to think about. When I see women and girls with their dad I am very happy for them. My dad has asked me countless times to forgive him and not hate him. I do not hate my dad and I have already forgiven him. No matter what he has done when he was not there for me, I don't look for an explanation, I don't try to make him feel guilty. I still accept him as my father and I want him to know that I do love him. But I also feel for him. Because he is a slave to the drug he chooses to do and I know he feels that there is no way out. I just think like what he had to be going through to make you want to do those things and he may feel like he cannot overcome. But I do know that he knows who God is. And I hope and pray that he will give his life to God and allow him to set him free. I'm happy for the ones who have that experience. I always wonder what is it like. It also saddens me to see that, because my dad never taught me anything or took the time out to spend time with me. I really wanted a relationship with my dad, I still do. Maybe one day when he is ready, I will be open to it. As a child and young adult, I never understood this. I always thought why me, how come I could not have a good daddy? It still breaks my heart.

Divorce

Divorce is never easy. When I went through my divorce it felt like someone had died because of all the sadness, trying to figure out where do I go from here. Trying to adjust to that person no longer being in my life. When you share children, pets, friends, it's hard. Everything reminded me of him at first. The shows that we watched together, the food we cooked together, the restaurants that we ate at, our home, sleeping, etc. The sleeping part was the hardest. I stayed woke for hours. Nights I could barely sleep. I was so used to sleeping next to him. I stayed up so late because I would hate to go to bed alone, I dreaded it. It always helped me sleep to feel him next to me, it made me feel safe. So, after everything I didn't want to watch those shows we used to watch together or whatever we did together, I did not want to do that anymore. I even stopped cooking for a long time. I was so depressed that

I stopped eating, and then it went to just eating oatmeal all day every day for weeks. I found comfort in oatmeal, for some reason. I guess because it was warm and it kept me full. I even stopped going to work for a short while. It was very hard. I had no interest in nothing, my mom even had to keep my children for a while. I had given up for that time. I just wanted to die because the pain was unbearable. I felt like my heart had been ripped from my chest. A broken heart is one of the worst feelings in the world. I was so grief stricken and then it became anger. I was so angry with God, because I thought I was doing everything right. I thought when a couple becomes married they find favor with the Lord. I started quoting scriptures back to the Lord because I was so angry with him. But as time went on God began to heal me little by little, day by day. My heart softened towards Him again. I started back reading, praying and praising His name.

Anyone who is thinking about divorce, going through a divorce, or your divorce just became final. Stay close to God. He heals all wounds. I was afraid of getting a divorce because I was ashamed if people found out my marriage did not work out. But I went through it because at the time I couldn't care about what others thought at the time, I had to do what was best for me. It was so many reasons why I did not want to get a divorce, but if I would have stayed then I would have not gotten the chance to be truly happy. I couldn't just stay for the children or the years we spent together, or what we had together. I had to think about if we are not truly happy together then we should both go our separate ways, and that is what we did. I don't have nothing bad to say about this man. He is a good man and we are still friends till this day but we were just not meant to be together.

I am not encouraging divorce at all. Please if you have questions or concerns about divorce please read the bible it talks about divorce. But to any one that is thinking about getting married or that is married, marriage is very serious to God. So please when you are looking for a mate make sure that it is someone you know you can spend the rest of your life with. Don't marry anyone because of how they look or because you know that they will take care of you, or because it seems like the right thing to do at the time. That is the wrong reason to marry. Do you really love that person, do that person love you? Is that person genuine? If you are already married, remember why you married that person and talk about your problems to each other and be honest with that person and try to make things work before you get a divorce.

Fibromyalgia

Dealing/living with fibromyalgia is one of the most difficult things I have to deal with. In the beginning, bad days for me I was not able to get out of bed, the pain was so severe all over with stiff joints. After learning about what I had, I learned how to prepare for bad days or just avoid them. I had to change my eating habits. Some foods or ingredients triggered my pain. Even with healthy food choices I have to deal with other triggers as well. Like stress, fright, no sleep, and weather. Any stress causes me to hurt. Anytime I cry my body will start hurting. Anytime I am frightened, like if a car pulls out in front of me in traffic, it feels like my body goes into shock and I immlitaly start hurting all over. If I don't get enough rest I will become stiff and will be in pain. Somedays I feel very fatigue. It feels like if I don't rest now or take a nap I will pass out. I have to know my limits, what I can do and what I can't do. If I push myself too much when I'm already tired or very busy and on the go, I will pay for it later, with pain. If you have ever heard me say well I have to take a nap before I do that, this is why. Rest and naps are important because it recharges my body, and sometimes the pain goes away. But I believe that God puts his hands on me when I am still and gives me the energy I need.

Even when taking pain meds, maybe after a month or so it stops working, because my body has become immune to it.

Another thing that triggers my fibro pain is the stormy weather. Although, I do enjoy the rain. The stormy weather didn't bother me at first but now it does. When it is very cloudy before it rains, I hurt so bad. Such severe pain it feels like my body is being crushed and it takes my breath away. It's so bad it makes me want to cry. But as soon as it starts to rain it eases up.

I've been told that exercise and stretching will help. I workout often. But when I work out and I get those muscle aches it hurts ten times worse for me. So it's kinda a struggle because I have to limit myself or stop some days. Either I endure the pain or stop.

Who Are You

After my divorce people kept telling me to focus on myself and find myself. This always made me mad because I felt like why do people keep telling me this. Even if you are fresh out of high school, just got a divorce, midlife crisis, etc. Finding yourself is important. After my divorce I spent so much time alone. I didn't have a choice but to find myself and on focus on myself. I struggled with this at first because I didn't want to be alone with me. I always tried to be around friends or always on the phone with someone. Then one day I just tried it and practiced it. I started writing in a diary of my pain each day. I started going for walks alone at the park, watching movies alone, eating out alone, etc. I also started to think about what do I like. What do I want in life, what are my goals? Who am I? What makes me, me? I also had to look deep inside myself and think about why am I the way I am. What are the things that people don't like about me that makes them uncomfortable and not want to be around me? The main thing was my attitude. So, I began to ask God to help me change that and practice changing my ugly ways, and change the things about me for the good. As time went on I began to enjoy my own company, I enjoyed being alone at home doing nothing. The number of friends I used to spend time with changed. It bothered me at first but, after a while I was used to it and it didn't bother me anymore. My life became so much more peaceful. Some of us do find happiness in a love one, family or friends. But it is very important to find happiness in your own self. Please, I encourage you, if you are not happy with yourself this could cause more problems for you. You can miss out on blessings or people simple may not want to be around you. What I learned is that people who are not happy with themselves sometimes cause problems for others, put down others, and trouble follow them (evil spirits). So, ask yourself, who am I? Am I happy with myself?

Chapter 2

Praises Go to You

To be close to God is to know Him. How do we usually get to know someone? We spend time with them, and we talk to them. Reading the Bible is one of the best ways to get to know God. The Bible tells us all about God. Who He is, what He does, what he likes and what He hates. Not only that, it lets us know that God is not a man. He cannot and will not lie. He is faithful and true. If you don't already know God, let me introduce Him.

Who Is He

Who is he, who still accepts me, as broken as I can be
After the sins I committed,
After being angry with Him
Even walking away, to go do my own thing
Who is He?
Welcoming me with open arms
Even after leaving Him, He caused me no harm,
He protected me still
All He has done for me,
How can I not do His will
Even through my ugly ways
His beautiful light somehow shines through me
Who is He?
He forgives me time and time again
Giving me more chances than I deserve to make things right
Who is He?
That calls me friend
Many times, I did not acknowledge Him
Refused to talk with Him
He still said I will be everything you need
He is my Redeemer
My Way maker
My Everything
The Forgiver of my sins
My Father
My friend
My healer
My comforter
Who is He?
Greater is He that is in me, than he that is in the world
Elohim

Jehovah

Jehovah Rapha: The Lord that heals
Jehovah Shammah: The Lord is there
Jehovah Jireh: The Lord will provide
Jehovah Shalom: The Lord of peace
Jehovah Sabaoth: The Lord of hosts

Jehovah Rapha
The Lord that heals
He heals me from all hurt and pain
When He heals me, His strength I gain
Jehovah Rapha
The ultimate healer
He can heal any disease
He will bind my wounds and heal my broken heart
Any time I am hurting he is never far apart

Jehovah Shammah
The Lord is there
Jehovah is everywhere
He is there when I am sleeping, watching me as I wake
Jehovah Shammah
Is with me at all times
He is always close by wiping my tears when I cry
I can't see Him but I know He is there
Jehovah Shammah is everywhere

Jehovah Jireh
The Lord will provide
He provides my wants and needs

He always makes a way for me
Every need I have, has already been met
There is nothing that I need that I can't get
Jehovah Jireh
My provider
He provides me with His grace and mercy and His unconditional love
He also provides His forgiveness, one thing that I need the most

Jehovah Sabaoth
The Lord of Hosts
He has an army of angels that protect us daily
He has the largest army of angels and of men
The devil thinks he can beat Jehovah, he better think again
He will not win
Jehovah Sabaoth
The Lord of hosts,
He does not need help
He has the power of life and death

Jehovah Shalom
The Lord of peace
The Lord gives me peace like no one else can
He walks with me daily and He holds my hand
I am not afraid and I do not fear
Because, I know my God Jehovah Shalom is here
He gives me peace in my heart and peace in my mind
Because, His promises are so divine
Jehovah Shalom
My peace
The world is chaotic and full of noise
But I can't see the chaos or hear the noise

I am so focused on you
You said that you are the one I need to bring all my problems to
Jehovah

I AM

Do you ever think about why God calls Himself I Am? The name "I Am" is in the Bible over 300 times. This is how God introduced Himself to Moses. God told Moses to tell the people that I Am has sent Him.

When I think about the name I Am, I think about the things that God has said like *"I am* the Alpha and Omega, says the Lord God, who is and who is to come the almighty" (Revelation 1:8).

I am the vine, you are the branches, whoever abides in me and I in him, he bears much fruit, for without me you can do nothing.

Fear not for *I am* with you, be not discourage for I am your God; I will strengthen you, I will uphold you with my righteous right hand (Isaiah 41:10).

God can be whatever we need Him to be
He is our joy, peace, and love
If you need a friend, talk to Him, He is listening
He can also be money if we need money.
God said that He will give you rest.
God is my everything
Who wouldn't want to serve a God like I AM
If you need a doctor, He can heal you.
If you are lost and don't know who you are I AM is your identity
Find out who you are in Him.
I AM is a part of us
He calls Himself I AM because He is

The Lord Provides

2 Peter 1:3

As His divine power has given to us all things that pertain to life and godliness, through the knowledge of Him who called us by his own glory and excellence.

God has already given us everything that we need. His grace, His forgiveness, and His presence. God gave us everything that we needed when he made the earth. Food, water, and shelter. The greatest thing He left with us is His love. No one can beat God's giving. No one can beat God's love. His love covers a multitude of sins.

"Every need that we have, has already been met."

Not only does God care about our needs; he will also bless you with your heart's desires.

But seek first the kingdom of God and his righteousness, and all these things will be added to you (Matthew 6:33).
Delight yourself in the Lord, and he will give you the desires of your heart (Psalm 37:4).

El Shaddai

Sometimes I'm at a loss for words when I think of you. The Creator of the universe, God almighty. The lovely sunrises and sunsets you display are absolutely breathtaking each day. Amazed at your ways, the things you do, is a great mystery that makes me fall more in love with you. The way you feed the animals and take care of their needs each day. Not just the animals, you have supplied our every need as well.

Even loving me during my unclean ways. I sin against you knowingly and you still stay. You wait for me to change, you have more patience than forever. I love you, God, not just because of your love for me, because of your love for all humanity. When I am alone sometimes I can feel your presence. It is such a good feeling. I feel safe, I feel wanted, and I feel satisfied. I love being in your presence. I love being alone with you. When I'm not alone, and when my spirit is down I long for you. Can't wait to get back to the feeling that rejuvenates my soul. God, your presence is the only presence that makes me feel whole.

But God

I can remember times when I couldn't walk,
But God carried me.
Times I couldn't even open my mouth to speak,
only could make a noise,
But God spoke for me
I can remember times when I struggled
to let go of bad relationships God forced me.
There were times when I couldn't see my way
But when the dust settled, God showed me
I can remember being so hurt, so broken, I felt worthless
But God healed and comforted me.
I can remember being in a room full of people and I felt so alone
But God reminded me that I was never alone
I can remember times when I was so lost, I didn't know myself.
All I wished for was death.
But God sent his son to rescue me.
When I poured my heart out and surrendered, He set me free.

Dear Heavenly Fatherly,

Thank you for giving me the opportunity to know you and to be able call upon your name. God, thank you so much for everything that you do for me. Help me to acknowledge your presence every day. Help me to be more like you each day. I just want to be pleasing and acceptable in your sight. I want to spend more time with you, God. Please put the desire in my heart to spend that time with you, and I pray that the desire will never go away. God, please open my eyes to the things that I may be blind to. Whether it is situations, people, or needs that I have not met. Please help me to die out to the flesh each day so that the will that you have for my life will be done. In Jesus' name, I pray, Amen.

Chapter 3

Deliver Me from Sins and Secrets

I can remember a time when I was so happy. Finally thought I conquered having bad thoughts about myself or just in general. In the midst of me thinking that I was delivered. I began to ask God to send me someone I could share my happiness with. Out of nowhere, I met this special guy. After talking to him and getting to know him I thought surely this is the one, God has answered my prayers. In the midst of dating this guy, I began to feel bad about myself again. I hated myself, I wanted to die. It was like I was going back to my old ways. That same negative mindset. Now how could this happen if I was delivered? I don't think that we are truly delivered from certain things until we are tested by God and passed the test. This relationship with this guy was my test and I kept failing daily. No matter what that person was saying or doing to me. I had to know in my own mind who I was. I had to know, no matter what was said that I was still worthy. I was still deserving. I am still a child of God. If that person was being unfair, difficult, not loyal, doesn't mean it was my fault or that I should hate myself just because our relationship wasn't working out. It took me a long time to realize that I was not the problem. Even if you are the cause of any problem, realize it, accept it, and ask for forgiveness and change things.

I believe that God tested me in this area of self-pity and self-hate because it's like a disease. It is very hard to get rid of and to stop it. Especially if you have done this for so long. Not only do I think it is a disease but it is also a sin to have such pity for oneself. Having self-pity causes you to focus so much on yourself that you forget about God and His promises. That He will uplift you, He will save you, and He will be with you. Sometimes I think that we are comfortable being there that it has become the norm for us. I think that we get comfortable in different sins and that makes it so hard for us to change. Especially trying to change it on or own, it will always be hard and impossible to change without the help of the Lord. We can be happy in the time of our storms. We just have to choose to be. Always look to God, remember who you are, and remember His promises. He has a plan for our life. To give us a future and a hope. He said that He will never leave us nor forsake us. A cure for self-pity is to draw closer to God.

Jeremiah 29:11: "For I know the plans I have for you," declares the LORD, "plans to prosper you and not to harm you, plans to give you hope and a future."

Deuteronomy 31:8: "It is the Lord who goes before you. He will be with you; he will not leave you or forsake you. Do not fear, do not be dismayed."

Father in Heaven,

Thank you so much for not treating me as though my sins deserve. Thank you, God, for your grace and mercy. I pray, Lord, from this moment forward I will not have self-pity or put myself down. I pray that no matter what comes my way I will look to you. I will remember your promises. I know that you are with me and will never leave me. I pray that you will always comfort me during difficult times. Help me to always know that I am worthy and loved. In Jesus' name, I pray, Amen.

What Does He See

Pain, heartaches, broken, depressed,
Misery is my ministry
Many nights I went to bed feeling defeated.
But God always woke me up to start me on my mission.
So many times, I wanted to give up but God said keep going.
Wondering what does God see in me that I can't see?
A woman once told me every morning that I wake,
God is smiling down on me.
Still wondering what is it that He sees in me.
He looks beyond my beauty,
He looks beyond brains
He looks beyond my faults
God said if you don't give up on me I won't give up on you.
Sometimes I did want to give up and walk away
I didn't want to see another day
Many nights I needed someone to listen
No one was there
Many times, I needed a shoulder to cry on,
But no one was there
But God was still there,
Waiting on me
He said I care
God said try me, trust me, lean and depend on me and you will see
how different your life will be
Then God whispers to me, I see a heart that will love me.

Why

Many times, I question God
Why me? What did I do to deserve this?
Why am I alive? Do you care?
I thought you said that you wouldn't put more on me than I can bear
What about that?
Are you listening?
Are you even there?
Times I even got angry with God
But I try not to get sassy with Him
Because he knows what is best
I do not want to cut off the supplier of my needs
I hear God saying be angry but sin not.
I imagined myself falling to my knees at His feet.
He gets up from His throne and He comforts me
He says abide in me, and I will abide in you.
Things will not be easy, but I am here for you
In whatever you may go through
Your greater doesn't have to be later
The peace I give starts today
The joy that I give lasts always
The love I have for you
Is never ending
No, I will not put more on you than you can bear
Are you listening?
I told you that I care.
You ask these questions because your ways are not my ways
And my thoughts are higher than yours.
Focus on me and I will be your peace.

Going Through

Your going-through will get you to
What you have been praying for
Your going-through will get you to your heart's desire
Your going-through will prepare you
For what God has for you.
Along the way do not ask
Why me? Am I being punished? What did I do wrong?
Don't give up, don't quit,
Please, don't go back to your old ways
Praise God, be patient, be still and know that He is God
Acknowledge Him
Talk with Him,
He is waiting to hear from you
Pray continuously
Believe in what you are praying for.
Know that you are loved
God will never leave you or forsake you
He brought you too far to leave you
He knows what you need
Your darkest hour is right before dawn.

God, Please

God, please have mercy on me
Please show me things I don't understand or can't see
Please forgive me for being me
God, please save a spot in Heaven for me
God, sometimes it seems like I just can't get it right
Please, God, be my guiding light
God, I just can't see my way
But I am trusting in you to make a way
I will not be fearful
I will not be sad
Please forgive me for the times I've acted out when mad
I get so confused and want to give up
Sometimes I just don't know what to do
God, please, I am giving this to you

God Speaks

I see you, I hear you
I know what you are going through
When waiting, I am near you
You are mine, you can't run from me
Be still, I will take care of you
Know that I am God
Trust and believe in me
I love you, I created you
I will not forsake you
When you cry I am holding you
When you are asleep, I protect you
When you need me I am there
Never think that I don't care
I know that you can't see me
But if you get real quiet and still
And wait on me, you will hear me

Here I Am

I'm headed back to the King
I don't know why I left
I promised you, God, that I will serve you until my death
I hope you will let me back in the Kingdom
I promise, God, this time I will stay
You said that you will forgive me for all my sins
and wipe my tears away
This world is a place of pain and sorrow
I've been waiting for that joy that they say will come tomorrow
I've been searching for peace,
But the last time I found peace was right here at your feet
Heavenly Father, please forgive me for my sins
I've been wrong, Father, in my life,
This time you win
I can't do this alone, not again
Father, I need your help
I give up
Life without you is rough
I love you, Father, Son, and the Holy Ghost
Queen J is here to stay

It's been a long time coming
God has brought me through so many storms and pain
Even when I can't see my way
I already know He has made a way
I said it's been a long time coming
And God is not through with me yet
I had so many ups and downs
But for every down God has turned it around
And for every tear that I have cried
Jesus was by my side
It's been a long time coming
I still have a long way to go
But I just want you to know that
God is good
Taste and see that He is good.

Deliver Me

Deliver me from my secrets so that I might find peace
Don't let my tormentors torment me
Please don't let my past haunt me
Deliver me from my ugly ways, show me better days
Deliver me from myself because, I know that the wages of sin is death
Deliver me from temptation and set me free
The place I'm in now, is not where I want to be
God, I need your help with this
Deliver me from all my distress
Deliver me from my ungodly desires
Help me to die out to the flesh each day
Change my ways that are not pleasing to you
God, I know I am my biggest enemy
Again, God, I ask, please set me free

Dear God,

Please continue to deliver me. Please, I do not want to become a slave to my sins. Please help me die out to my flesh so that I may not sin against you, God. Please, Father, don't leave me nor forsake me. I really need you, God. My heart is broken and my spirit is crushed. You said in your word that you are close to the brokenhearted and you save those who are crushed in spirit. God, I need to feel your presence, Lord. Please come see about me and heal my broken heart. God, I need you. Deliver me from myself, and all my distress. Sometimes I feel lost, and feel like giving up. God, deliver me from all my pain and anguish. God, please hover over me and deliver me and set me free. In Jesus' name, I pray, Amen.

Letting Go

When the enemy comes in like a flood,
when it looks like nothing will go right
when the pain is unbearable
when you become so confused you don't know what to do
when you ask yourself, how did I get here or
what did I do to deserve this

Run to God, cry out to God, pray multiple times a day. Ask others to pray for you, praise God's name. Believe that things will get better, trust in God. Sometimes the things we go through help us to let go of somethings that may be hurting or hindering us. It prepares us for what we have been praying for, and what we deserve. When we are forced to let go of certain things or people it hurts more. We may have allowed a person to hurt us too many times. Or if we are forced to let go of a sin or a bad habit, it may have embarrassed us, caused us to hit rock bottom, caused us to get hurt, or just made us feel bad about ourselves. If you know something or someone is hurting you or isn't good for you, let it go before things get too deep. Pray and ask God to help you let it go.

Jehovah Jireh,

Please help me to let go of the people/things that are hurting me. Please heal me from these things. Give me the strength to rise above them, give me the strength to heal from them, and to overcome. Help me to resist the temptation of these things/people. Dear God I really need you, I can't do this on my own.

In Jesus name, Amen

Chapter 4

Speak Over Yourself
Be Encouraged and Not Discouraged

When I look back over this year
There was some good and bad.
But God was with me every step of the way.
There were times when I couldn't see my way.
Times where I thought I would go crazy.
Times where I didn't want to go on anymore
I wanted to give up, I was at my lowest
But God stepped in and reached out his hand
He spoke to me.
I will be your strength, I will be your joy,
I am your peace, lean and depend on me
Sometimes I got so caught up in what I was going through,
I forgot all about who God was.
I made a vow to myself to never feel
worthless, unwanted, and unloved.
I know that trouble will still come and there
may come a time when my spirit may get crushed again
But I will remember my God and who He is.
He is my deliver, my way maker, my redeemer,
and the lover of my soul.
So, no matter who doesn't want me or,
Who stops loving me today, God will still love me tomorrow
No matter how big my problems may seem
God is still God and He is in control
He saved me before and He will save me again
He doesn't just do it for one person, He does it for all.
Nothing is too little or too great for God.

I Believe in Me

When I am weak, then I am strong
Because God is my strength
I am worthy,
Because the highest price paid for anything was paid for me
I am love
Because God's love is unconditional and it will last for all eternity
I am beautiful
Because God made me in his image of how He wanted me to be.
Fearful and wonderfully made
I am enough
Because God accepts me just as I am
Flaws and all
I am amazing
Because even when I'm not thinking of Him, He is always thinking of me
I was on His mind before I was even born
I am free
Because God sent His son to die for me
I am Queen
Because I embrace all that I am
I know who He is and all that He can be.
I also know that He lives on the inside of me
Without Him I am nothing
With Him I am everything that I can be.

You Are Loved

No matter how many times you've been rejected
No matter how many times you heard the word no!
Don't give up, don't put yourself down
Even if you think you are not good enough
You are still worth it.
You still deserve the best
Even if your dream has not come true yet
Keep holding on to faith and don't lose hope
As much as you doubt yourself
Or, whatever you are waiting for, have that much hope in God
Believe that God will and He is
God is the Great I AM. He will never fail you.
Maybe it's just not time yet
God does everything on His timing and not ours.
He is saving the best for last. No matter how much time has passed
Please think nothing but the best of yourself
No matter how many mistakes that you made or
How bad someone else has treated you
God still loves you
He thinks that you are special
I know you may feel alone and you may not have any friends.
But you don't need any friends to be great
Remember when you are lonely, God is still there
God is not going anywhere
Acknowledge Him.
Spend as much time as you can with Him
Get wrapped in His love. Run to God; He will embrace you.
God's love is the best love, because it is overwhelming

I Will Not Be Sad

I will not be sad
Life itself is tough, rough, and not fair,
I had to face my biggest fears and yet I'm still here.
They say time heals all wounds but
God mended my broken heart, he has healed me,
I will not be sad because I know my God rejoices over me
He watches over me, He protects me,
He loves me, with his unconditional love
He keeps me. I am kept by the keeper
I can't think of anything greater than knowing God
Knowing that almost no matter what you do and where you go
He is always by your side
My God, My God
I will not be sad
It is said to rejoice in this day that you have made.
I will do just that
I will keep my eyes on you so that I may not fall
I will dwell in the shelter so that I may abide in His shadows
I will not be sad because I know who God is and what He can do

Sometimes I often felt like I wasn't good enough for certain people. Maybe I was too much or not enough. I had to realize that it wasn't always me. Sure, we all could use a little more self-improving. Yes, some of us do have bad habits. If someone continues to point out the bad things about you, take some time out to think about this, is this constructive criticism, is this person trying to help, or is this person just being negative? Then take a step back and evaluate yourself and the relationship you have with this person. I had to deal with this for a while, where this person always made me feel bad about myself. I was always beating myself up about the things I was doing wrong. Then I began to sink back into depression. I felt like how can I make this person happy and this person was not accepting me the way that I am. So it was a constant battle with myself trying to force myself to change how I had been for many years. Reminding myself how wrong I was. In reality I wasn't wrong about certain things. This person just wanted me to change how they thought things should be done or said. Doesn't mean I was wrong. What I had to learn was that no matter how someone felt about me if it was something negative, is to not beat myself up about it. One place I don't want to go back into is depression or a dark place. Sure, this person may not like this about me or maybe I use the wrong words, or maybe I exaggerate a little at times, etc. Doesn't mean I should hate myself or feel like I'm the reason something didn't work out. I'm not saying to get the big head and think yeah, I'm right and they are the wrong ones. What I'm saying is to love yourself enough to know when to evaluate yourself and the situation. Love yourself enough to never hate yourself and always love yourself no matter what someone says about you.

God said that he would be our strength in our time of weakness. I always wondered how that was possible. One day he showed me how. In many times of weakness He gave me strength that I didn't know that

I had. But it wasn't me, it was all God. Before doing anything I sometimes whisper God give me strength to do this, or God be with me.

Many times I went nights with no sleep and got up and went to work. I felt like a zombie. Strength of God.

Many times I drove for miles struggling to stay awake, making it to my destination safely Strength of God. Times I didn't eat all day but was still able to do work, like cleaning, moving heavy objects, almost about to faint, but I did not. Strength of God. A few times I went months without eating my favorite foods or the things I eat everyday. This was not an easy thing to do, but I did it by the strength of God.

If you are thinking oh that's nothing I have done that plenty of times. I'm sure we all have but please know that, we only were able to do these things because of his grace, his mercy and his strength that we rely on each day just to roll out the bed sometimes, His strength we need desperately to keep calm and not lose it.

Chapter 5
You Are Strong

I Will Not Assist the Devil

I will not water the devil seeds that the devil planted for me.
He constantly tells me I'm a failure
Reminds me of my past, always whispers in my ear,
I will always be last
He keeps reminding me of things that I can't grasp
Satan is the author of confusion. He wants us to stay confused.
He wants us to lose.
He always tries to suppress knowledge the best way he can.
Never believe anything the devil speaks
He has no power, he is weak.
Only way he can win, if you assist him, by giving into sin
The devil will never tell you the truth
He is the father of lies
He laughs when someone cries
Devil, I'm not writing this to acknowledge you
But to remind you that, you may win a few battles
When we shed a tear
But you will never win the war.
Every mind and everything you try to destroy God will restore
You may be running rapid now,
And you keep bringing up my past,
because I already know your future.

Sometimes the enemy knows who you will become before we even realize who we are. He knows the power we have and what gifts we possess. So, he will start early in our lives to try and stop us from being who God wants us to be, by telling us lies. He tells us lies about ourselves or tries and tricks us off the right path and tells us things like God isn't real. Or no one loves you or, why would God allow bad things to happen to us or anyone? There are a number of lies that the enemy will try to manipulate us and have us to walk away from God. The enemy does not single anyone out unless you are already on his side. If you have children, the enemy will try to get to your children early when they begin to understand things more. Please continue to pray for them and speak good things over them. Do you remember as a child, a teenager, a young adult, the lies he has told you? I do and it stuck with me for years. Please don't call your children names, always show them love each day. Let them know that they are loved each day. Pray with them, talk to them about God. Remember, we have a choice of who we will serve, God or Satan. Teach and show your children who God is so that they will choose to serve God also. I'm not trying to tell you how to raise your children but, I am just trying to encourage you to tell them you love them often, welcome them with love, and open that door of communication with them. I did not have this growing up. If I did I do believe my life would have been a little bit better. I do not discredit my mom in any way. I do know that she loved me. She is a good mom. But again, if I did have more love shown to me I do believe I would have made better choices and not going around looking for love in all the wrong places. Not only that but I didn't know who I was, I was lost, and I did not know my worth. Listening to the enemy and getting far from God. Sometimes we will listen to one or two lies from Satan rather than believe and hold on to over 3,000 promises God has promised us. If you are anything like I was, I would always think, I would never win anything, or I don't deserve this, because of the bad things I done. Or I am a nobody, I don't mean anything to anyone. If you think like this or have any negative thoughts about yourself, please stop. Those are lies from the enemy. Know that you deserve any good thing that comes from God.

James 1:17: Every good gift and every perfect gift is from above, coming down from the Father of lights, with whom can be no variation, neither shadow that is cast by turning.

Always remember who you are in Christ. Who you are in Christ and who you are period is one of the most important titles you will ever have. And the only title that will last. Always know that you are a child of God, you are chosen, you are a king/queen, a little lower than the angels, blessed, forgiven, and a friend. The list goes on.

Just knowing who you are should make you feel a whole lot better about yourself. Once you know who you are you are not lost anymore.

Who we are in Christ no one can ever take from us. I'm telling you, it may not sink in at first but continue to read scriptures, recite them over and over.

Say this out loud: I am someone, I am loved, I am chosen, and I am worthy.

Your attitude should change about yourself. If you are still having trouble with this ask God to open your eyes and show you. Also ask God to open your eyes to things you may be blind to. Ask Him to remove the veil and He will. Sometimes we can be blind to certain things because we may be too deep in sin. We have to change our way of thinking. Ask God to do this for you. Try this, it worked for me. I got a picture of me in my phone and went to photo edit and it allows you to write on the picture in different colors. So, I wrote these words around my picture: *Beautiful, worthy, strong, amazing, smart, good enough, and loving.* Whatever you need to do to change your mind about yourself go for it.

Dear God,

Help me to see that I was made in your image. Help me to love and accept myself more and more each day. In the midst of learning how to love myself please don't allow me to become bigheaded or think more of myself than I ought. Lord, change my mindset about how I see myself. I pray that you will help me through this. I am nothing without you, but with you I know I can be all that I can be. In Jesus' name, I pray, Amen.

During a time of depression (my depression comes in seasons), it could last a year, half a year, or a month. Depending on how long I wanted to hold on to it. At one point I did not see a reason to live anymore. Life was not worth living to me. I wanted to die every day. Sometimes I didn't want to wake up, and I would always dread going to sleep. I would stay up for hours and would never get in bed because I was depressed about going to bed alone, including other things. But I once heard someone say, "If Jesus died for us, then who are we to decide when we are to die?" I also heard Him say, "I have given you three reasons to live: Marie, Alexander, and Joseph Michael." I can imagine Him saying, "What about me? Am I not enough for you? Are we not enough for you to live?" When I heard this this changed my mind. Don't focus on your failures, focus on how great God is.

Philippians 4:14: I can do all things through Christ who strengthens me.

Isaiah 41:10: Fear not, for I *am* with you; be not dismayed, for I *am* your God. I will strengthen you, I will uphold you with my righteous right hand.

Isaiah 40:31: But those who wait on the Lord shall renew *their* strength; They shall mount up with wings like eagles, They shall run and not be weary, They shall walk and not faint.

2 Corinthians 12:9: And He said to me, "My grace is sufficient for you, for my strength is made perfect in weakness."

Heavenly Father,
Give me the strength to make it through each day.
Help me from feeling overwhelmed with the things
that are weighing me down. Give me the strength
to keep going when I want to give up. Help me to
keep my eyes on you so that I will not fall. Please,
God, make me steadfast and unmovable like the tree
that is planted by the water. God, give me the
strength and the courage to speak over my own self.
God, please build me up and mold me into the person you want me to be. In Jesus' name, I pray, Amen.

Regaining Your Strength

Sometimes we may think that just because we haven't given up and we are still living, it makes us strong. Yes this is true, but let's talk about some things that make us strong.

- Patience

  God said for us to not be anxious about anything. Not being patient makes us weak because if haven't seen the fruits of our labor we get discouraged. God also says don't get weary when doing good. When we are waiting, we can begin to start to doubt God, we may break down. We may even say I give up or I don't even want that anymore. So when we think and talk this way we become weak or even have a weak moment. (This is normal because we are human.) But without faith it is impossible to please God. It is impossible to doubt and believe in God at the same time.

- Be optimistic

  Always hope for the best. Try to smile even though your heart may be crying. Learn how to be happy with life now and for the things you do have. I know sometimes it is hard but it is always good to be optimistic. As long as we have God, then there is always hope.

- Control your temper

  Don't lose your temper. Being able to have self-control in every situation makes us stronger. Majority of us get mad. Which is okay to get mad but the Bible says get angry and sin not. When we get angry it is best to control ourselves and not blow up, yell, tear things up, call people names, or take things out on other people. We have to learn to deny our flesh by not giving in and acting out. Deny your flesh by not getting even or by letting people know you are mad by destroying things or just stomping around and slamming stuff down. Some of us love to get even when people have done us wrong. But we are not to repay evil for evil. God says vengeance is mine, he will repay back for what is done.

- Learn from your mistakes
  We can become strong by learning from our mistakes. If we keep making the same mistakes, it will make us weak. Making the same mistakes will make you weak because you are not learning but going in circles. We all may be repeating a cycle or doing things we know we shouldn't be doing. I know this can be hard to stop certain cycles. I continued a cycle for many years. This is kind of like the Israelites, their eleven-day journey caused them forty years because they didn't listen to God and started doing their own thing. Can you imagine praying for something and not getting it until ten years later because you wanted to go your own way? When you could have been blessed sooner if you would have just listened and obeyed God. I made up my mind that I do not want to be like that. If I can be blessed with things now just by obeying God. Instead of going through so much heartache and pain of going through an unhealthy cycle when I can just do right the first time around and it not take years and years.

- Control your emotions
  Don't let your emotions make your decisions for you. Don't make certain decisions because you are mad or just emotional and they may not be a decision you would have made if you

were not mad. Don't get caught up on bad emotions. Don't focus on being sad, mad, depressed, or worried. These emotions can make us weak. Also, if we are deep in these emotions for a long period of time it can become a doorway for bad spirits to use us or influence us.

We are all waiting on something. Whether it is our circumstances, weight loss, hair growth, strength, healing, a raise, looking for a home, a spouse, a change in others, a job, a baby to be born, Godly power, hearing God's voice, etc. Whatever we are waiting for it is a process that takes time. During this waiting period we should know that God is waiting on us as well. Know that we can talk to Him during this time. Cast all your cares unto Him. Be specific in what you are requesting. Whatever you are asking for ask that you will be able to handle it. Ask that He help you to be patient while waiting. Also give thanks in advance.

I say that God is waiting on us because if God would bless us so quickly or if He blessed us in a way where we did not have to wait, we would appreciate Him less. If God gave us everything we asked for as soon as we asked, we would probably be doing whatever we wanted and not obeying his word. Some things we may ask for it may not be time for us to have that, because we may not be in a place in life when we are mature enough to be responsible for certain things. Waiting and being patient builds character. When it comes to asking God for certain things we have to obey God. We cannot live any kind of way and expect God to bless us. Sometimes He may be waiting on us to change our ways and spend more time with Him. He could be waiting on us to let go of a grudge or to tell someone I am sorry, I apologize. Or He could be waiting on us to be more loving, and friendly. Everyone we come across is not always a stranger. They could very well be an angel and we may not even be aware of it. So always treat others with kindness, they could be just like us, feeling broken and worthless or just going through this difficult journey called life. We never know what people are going through. Some people may show it on their faces by looking non-approachable, or they can be hiding behind a smile sometimes just like we are. It doesn't cost a thing to be kind.

What to Do when You Are Going Through

We all are going through something or have been through something. And we are all hurting from something; no one is perfect. We can be healed from all pain whether it is in this life or the next life, God will heal all pain if you give it to Him. And with the help of God whatever you are going through God will always see us through. Going through can mean a variety of things.

- Grieving

  You could be dealing with a passing of a loved one. Or maybe you are going through a divorce. Going through a divorce feels like someone has died. The marriage has died. But it could be different for some people; they feel free.

- Depression

  Depression comes in all forms where you can be depressed about anything.

- Losses

  People can go through different losses. The loss of a job, a house, car, relationship/friendship.

- Bad diagnosis

  Being diagnosed with a disease, cancer, autoimmune disorder, etc. Or you could be going through all these things at one time. Maybe your situation is not listed or maybe you really haven't gone through anything yet. If not when that time comes and if you are going through now, I assure you this will help you.

Always keep the faith in God. Believe that there will be a better outcome. Know that God will never leave you or forsake you. Speak over yourself. Forgive others, give more. Give a little, get a little. Give a lot, receive a lot. Not saying let people take advantage of you or donate to every charity but be a blessing to others unexpected sometimes. Make someone smile by smiling more. Just give out of the kindness of your heart. Tell someone to keep the change. Be obedient. Remember God and His promises daily. Spend more time with him daily. I know we are all busy and have hectic schedules sometimes, but try to spend at least 30 minutes a day with God. Do this for 30 days and see if something will change for you. In that 30 minutes you can read the Bible, pray, sing praises to His name, or whatever you would like to do. If you don't have 30 minutes maybe try to 10 or 15 minutes. If you do this for thirty straight days it will become a habit for you. If you had the time to do this at the beginning of each day, you may even have a better day. God says to put Him first and not last. So starting this early would be great, maybe you would have to get up a little earlier. I know all of our lifestyles are different, even if you can squeeze in this time throughout the day would be good as well.

Please know you don't have to limit yourself to only 30 minutes with God. You can spend as much time with him as you like. I go to have prayer at a church from time to time that may last up to 2 hours. That may seem like a long time to pray but, when I'm there the time flies by like you would not believe.

God is the only one who can deliver us, the only one who can heal us. He is the sender of each blessing. He told us to bring all our troubles to Him. Once you do this God will always make a way out of no way. Also remember when we are going through, when we are waiting every blessing and every deliverance does not come overnight.

Don't get Weary in well doing *(Galatians 6:9)*.
You are strong, where I am weak
When I am down, I wait for you to speak
You always make me feel better when I think about who you are
A mighty sovereign God
Who knows all and sees all.
A God who sits high and looks low. A God who will never say no.
You are the driving force in my life
When I am wrong you make me right
I thank you for the good times and the bad. I thank you for every-
thing that I have, from the smallest things
to the largest things that hold great value
I don't know where I would be or what I would do without you
(I don't want to know)
I thank you for growth and granting me with the ability to change.
I thank you for allowing me to be open-minded
and not to think the same way I used to think.
If I had 10,000 tongues I still could not thank you enough.
Lord, I thank you.

I know sometimes it is hard to be strong. Especially when a lot of people depend on you. Or if you just have a lot going on. Some people have hectic schedules and sometimes life can become overwhelming. If you have to do one more thing or one more bad thing happens you just want to give up, and you feel like you can't take it anymore, or you may have a breakdown. I know sometimes I have felt like this. I know I have always been the person who checks on family and friends and visits them often. But when my spirit is low from being over-whelmed, I don't reach out to people, sometimes I don't hear from the people in my circle. Before I have been accused of acting funny. When that was not the case. When I am down or overwhelmed I stay to myself. People will get used to you reaching out and once you miss a day or a weekend they think something is wrong. But they don't think something maybe wrong with the person. Like I may be sick or just not able to reach out because of stress or whatever the situation may be. Please, I encourage you, if you have not heard from a friend you usually hear from, please check on them, I know for me when I am MIA it's because I am dealing with something or I may need to clear my head, spend more time with God. When I do so much for people sometimes I feel drained. My spirit and body need to be re-stored and sometimes I need that quiet time to do so. I used to think wow, no one checks on me or cares about me. Or who can I call when I am going through or who is going to be there for me. I had to learn that if I'm here to be a little glimmer of light for people, listen to them vent, make them laugh, help them, pray for them, etc. What's wrong with that? As a servant of God that is one reason we are here. He said that we are the light and salt. To be here for each other. Even if I am here for people and it seems like no one is here for me, then that is okay because I do have God. I'll be the glimmer of light and God will be my sunshine. I do believe the people that are in my circle would do the same thing for me in return. People will not know what we

65

need or what we are going through unless you tell them. I know for me I would think I had no one because they may not have been available at that point in time. But when we are going through God sometimes is all we need. I have found out that if I go immediately in prayer or just simply talk to God I feel so much better. Especially when I can get somewhere quiet and pour my heart out. I feel like God is listening and whatever feeling I was feeling before has left. Sometimes when we are alone or do things on our own that is where our greatest strength comes. There are plenty of things we don't necessarily want to do on our own for the first time or anytime. But when we do something by force or we may not have a choice but to step out on faith, God is with us. He said where we are weak He will be our strength.

Chapter 6
Be Thankful

It is always important to give thanks. Especially to God. We ask so much of God each day. Do you ever say thank you? I believe God enjoys delivering us and protecting us, we are his children. God also wants us to be thankful and appreciative. When we give, He wants us to be cheerful about it. It does not have to be Thanksgiving for us to say what we are thankful for. Almost every time I pray I try to be thankful. Do you think God would be in a hurry to bless us or deliver us if we are never thankful or if we are ungrateful? This is so important. It may sound silly but sometimes we should be thankful for the bad times, the storms we went through because when we go through the storm most times we come out better people or maybe God has blessed us double for our trouble so yes, always be thankful. Sometimes when we are used to being a Negative Nancy when it may seem easier to focus on our troubles and feel sorry for ourselves. I used to love to have pity parties. But it was pointless because God did not get any glory out of it, and why continue to feel awful about something you probably can't change in that moment? When you get to this place stop and think about all the things God have already done for you. Start to say everything that you are thankful for. Almost every day I go home from work I thank God for my job, the car that I drive, and the home that I go home to. It may not be my dream car or my dream home that I would like but I am very thankful for them. I am thankful for that because they are doing everything that I need them to do. It gets me from one place to another and my house is my shelter. Amen. When you think about the things you are thankful for and just give God thanks in the bad times, your mood will change and you may come out of the storms a little bit faster or it may not even bother you.

I thank God for waking me up this morning and giving me songs of praise to sing. Many times I have asked God to please not wake me up because I didn't feel like I deserved to live, or my pain was just too much to bear. But the fact that he has woken me up again and again, Hallelujah! Brings tears to my eyes and I just have to say Lord I thank you.

Not only be thankful to God but take the time out to tell your family or your circle how much you appreciate them and how you are thankful for them and thankful for the role that they play in your life. Some people may really need to hear this. They may think that they are not needed or it may just make them feel good inside.

Ephesians 5:20: Giving thanks always for all things in the name of our Lord Jesus Christ to God, even the Father.

Luke 6:38: Give and it shall be given unto you; good measure, pressed down, shaken together, running over, shall they give into your bosom. For with what measure ye mete shall be measured to you again.

Psalm 100:4: Enter the gates with thanksgiving. And into his courts with praise: Give thanks unto Him, and bless His name.

Psalm 107:1: O give thanks unto Jehovah; for He is good; For His lovingkindness.

2 Corinthians 9:7: let each man do according as hath purposed in his heart: not grudgingly, or of necessity: for God loveth a cheerful giver.

I would like to thank the people and old friends that gave up on me, or just let our relationship/friendship go. It forced me to find myself and to find out who I am in Christ. It was all a challenging time but I think it was well worth it. I thank God for the good times and the bad times. The bad times are what made me. It made me uncomfortable and I knew I had to do something different to be in a place where I could be comfortable again. Comfortable the right way and not comfortable in sin. I thank God for the change and for the growth. I am not the same person I used to be, thank God of that. Sure, I still possess some same characteristics that make me who I am but my ways are far from being the same. I am at a place in my life now where I am set apart to live a life the way God would want me to live and focusing on being a better, happier, and healthier me.

Dear Lord,

Again I come to you just to say I thank you for every opportunity you have given me, every door you have opened. I thank you for every time that you have protected me, and thank you for still protecting me. I thank you for your grace and your mercy. Thank you God for giving me another chance to get things right with you. Lord, I thank you for your forgiveness, your love, and kindness. Thank you for being God.

In Jesus name Amen